BRITISH

designed to introduce the collections of the British
Museum to the widest possible audience. 12 individual
cards have been chosen to illustrate the named theme,
making these beautifully crafted numbered sets ideal as
gifts, for personal correspondence, for postcard
collectors and as educational source material.

For further information or to order contact:

BRITISH MUSEUM PRESS
A division of The British Museum Company Ltd
46 Bloomsbury Street
London WC1B 3QQ
Telephone 020 7323 1234
www.britishmuseum.co.uk

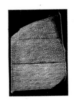

BRITISH MUSEUM ▥ PRESS

Price £4.50 inc VAT

ISBN 0-7141-1773-0

9 780714 117737

12 BRITISH MUSEUM POSTCARDS

Pectoral with a heart scarab in a barque
Polychrome glazed composition plaque. The scarab
naming its female owner Ptahemheb, flanked by a girdle
tie of Isis and a *djed*, is blessed by Isis and Nephthys.
Probably from Memphis, Egypt.
Nineteenth Dynasty, *c.* 1275 BC. Height 9.7cm. EA 7865.

THE BRITISH MUSEUM

Dancing girls, _detail_
Part of a banquet scene from the tomb of Nebamun.
Painted plaster. From Thebes, Egypt. Eighteenth Dynasty,
c. 1400 BC. Height of whole fragment 61cm. EA 37984.

THE BRITISH MUSEUM

The Gayer-Anderson Cat
Bronze cat from Egypt, c. 664–30 BC.
Presented by R.G. 'John' Gayer-Anderson (Pasha)
and Mary Stout. Height 38cm. EA 64391.
© 1985 Lee Boltin   P/C EA 35
Printed by Blue Cube Ltd. Denham Uxbridge UB9 5ED

The god Amen-Re
Head of a figure sculpted in the style of king Tutankhamun.
Black granite. Egypt, late Eighteenth Dynasty, c. 1330 BC.
Height of whole figure 148cm. EA 21.
Photograph by Peter Hayman

Shabti **of king Sety I**
Glazed composition *shabti* bearing the spell to cause it to
carry out agricultural work for its dead master in the Other
World. Egypt, Nineteenth Dynasty, *c.* 1279 BC.
Height 22.8cm. EA 22818.

Photograph by Peter Hayman

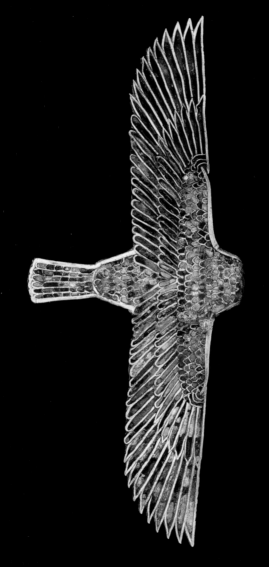

THE BRITISH MUSEUM

Pectoral of a flying falcon
Gold, in the round, its back once inlaid with red, blue
and green glass. Egypt, Saite Period or later, after 600 BC.
Width 14.8cm. EA 57323

Hippopotamus
Glazed composition decorated with aquatic plants.
Egypt, Middle Kingdom, c. 1900 BC.
Length 6.3cm. EA 59777

© 1986 The Trustees of the British Museum.   P/C EA 58
Printed by Blue Cube Ltd. Denham Uxbridge UB9 5ED